THE STARTLING LIGHT
OF BELONGING

First paperback edition April 2024
IF Press
314 Pleasant Ave
Alma, MI 48801
Cover and text designed by Joshua Zeitler
Cover illustrations by Gustave Doré

The Startling Light of Belonging

NEW & SELECTED POEMS

Lynn Rather

IF Press

Contents

II. Aubade 25

Foreword

Lynn Rather was a gardener, a collector of rocks and deep friendships, a recluse, a book collector, a spiritual seeker, a train enthusiast, a former lesbian separatist, a cat lover, a janitor, a mystic, a mystery I will be unraveling the rest of my life, and, of course, as evidenced by the book you hold in your hand, a poet.

And what a poet Lynn was! Her words strike straight to the heart of things as they are. To hear them in her voice was to part the veil between image and understanding, all in the space of a breath.

After a year-long struggle with cancer, Lynn passed to the next phase in her eternal journey on November 27, 2023, but her voice— her generosity, humility, gratitude, grace, and yes, even her bluntness—will echo in those who loved her for many decades to come. And now, I hope, in you.

These poems have hovered at the edge of my consciousness for months, reminding me of "our imperfect and uncertain / union with transcendence." These poems have shepherded me through grief in their frank grappling with mortality. These poems have lifted my chin to notice the clouds breaking. These poems have kept me company in those moments I am closest to and furthest from whatever god may be.

"Every spring I want to plant more," Lynn whispers. "I hardly ever do."

As an editor, I have tried to meddle as little as possible with the magic Lynn passed on to me. We began assembling these final works after many exhausting months of chemotherapy. I asked her for everything; I didn't want a piece of her to be lost. There were some poems that she expressed doubt about publishing, but I have included them because I felt they would tell the reader some otherwise neglected facet of her extraordinary personality and consciousness. If anything falls flat, it is my fault—but a fault born of love. I would have liked the arrangement to be a more collaborative process, as well, but I can only hope that I have proven worthy of the trust she placed in me.

She did, however, have a habit of not titling poems—a creative choice that I wanted to honor. That being said, because of formatting concerns, I felt it detracted from the impact of the collection. Any poem titled "Nocturne" or "Aubade" was the interference of my hand. My hope was to honor her engagement with poetic tradition (Lynn was an avid and prolific reader), as well as to provide a window into the text beyond a bracketed pre-statement of the first line, which oftentimes did not do justice to the subtle and sweeping moves in the body of the poem.

Finally, Lynn did not have a chance to write acknowledgments, but I want to acknowledge at least a few of those who were instrumental in supporting her in the creation of these poems, and in her final days. Most of all, I want to thank Patty, a dear friend who provided invaluable care and companionship. I want to thank Lynn's sister, Laurie Jeffay, who handled Lynn's affairs and was a welcome comfort to her, and her brother Philip Rather, whom she held dear. I want to thank Angie Kelleher for her constant friendship and encouragement. I want to thank Bob Vivian, whose presence and guidance she treasured. I want to thank all the attendees of the Rumi Hour, past and present, who shared and encouraged her love of poetry, but especially Michelle Lucchesi, Kathryn Starry, Susan

Priest, Randall Mead, and Joe Smolka. Finally, I want to thank Dawn Daniels, the proprietor of Ballyhoo Books and Brew, where Lynn spent so many hours, and on whose shelves her work will always have a home. There are so many other treasured friends that I'm sure Lynn would like to thank—so to all of you, near and far, thank you, thank you, thank you.

And to you holding this book, thank you for keeping her memory alive.

This is how we save ourselves
and each other

One poem at a time.

~Joshua Zeitler

The Startling Light of Belonging

New Poems

Do not sink into sadness, even though the mysteries
of the other world slip past you entirely.
There are plays within plays you cannot see.

~Hafiz

I've dreamt in my life dreams that have stayed with me
ever after... and altered the color of my mind.

~Emily Brontë

I. Nocturne

Nocturne (Wind)

the air turns to jello
and I am unable to move,
much less forward.
frozen in time,
I sit and smoke, sit and smoke,
thinking about gravity, dark energy,
and dark matter, watching
How the Universe Works.

outside,
the trees are loud with wind.
I want the wind to move me,
to carry me away
from judgment and expectation.
what if that wind
comes from somewhere inside?

Event Horizon

after the biopsy
October steams in like
an abandoned ghost freighter
all fog and rain and shadows

after the phone call
the floor falls away
galactic turmoil, grumble and groans,
continents collide, breaking glass,
whirlpools of feeling,

suddenly my furniture seems more real.
I'm in a dream I'm having
about my life,
carried down a river of fear,
hope like tiny life preservers
float beside me

Nocturne (Orbits)

brooding
a dark lake tugs the shore
under a sky studded with stars
I ask if miracles exist
I ask God for a sign
a small meteor perhaps
while miracles abound around me
the heron, the hummingbird,
the foxglove, moonlight dancing
on the water,
even the black flies biting,
our intersecting orbits
miracle enough

In the Hospital

where we walk a quad of halls
to pass some time
which folds in on itself

where compassion blooms
these people are in trouble

where we learn life skills
then go back to coloring

where a misty spirit visited
two nights in a row
(don't tell anyone about this)

where I wonder how I let this happen
and know the answer

where I say what they want to hear
so they'll let me go home

where the silence at night is a roar
that swallows one whole

depression and loneliness lie. Fear lies.
my shadow knows this somehow.

our stories tell stories
we don't even know

Nocturne (Union)

How did I miss this?
The awe of everyday life,
a filling awe, and gratitude.
Sometimes I'm moved to tears,
other times I wander dark rooms
amidst our imperfect and uncertain
union with transcendence.

The Bend

I went round the bend
and stood there wondering

I went astray and didn't come back
'til two years from now

I went home and my bedroom exploded

I went for a walk
and the trees were on fire

I went up north and was quiet
and the stars shone down

Nocturne (Mirror)

She wades through her day
as if through jello
All directions seem futile
while she waits for test results

She feels the loss
of family and friends
how hard it is for them

She says though death isn't imminent
it's in the rearview mirror
objects are closer than they appear

She wonders about dying
will it be easy or hard?
will it be a grand adventure?

She wonders about other realms and dimensions

She is somewhat excited

In the Distance

in the distance a train whistle
under a frozen sky
stars timeless and shining
a winter night moves on
it is freezing

more real than waking life
I dream of friends long dead
and we talk for ages

Nocturne (Tenant)

I am a tenant of broken places,
cancer and uncertainty.
It feels strange
to part with belongings,
a life emptying,
what to save, what to discard
or give away.
Shadows lengthen across the yard.
There are other moves
not so distant now.

The Far Lands

noisy crows afoot in the yard
snowstorm coming
the long winter wait and endless grey
I inhabit a frozen place
I feel lost
and move through my days
like a glacier
after the radiation and chemo
where is the next step?
what direction to take?
what does a future mean now?
I dream of the far lands
where everything is
as you'd like it to be
wide and open, like survival
or a field of sunflowers
following the sun across the sky

Nocturne (Light)

the moon rises on one white wing
night puts on her dark coat
and all across the county
yard lights snap on
like some earthbound galaxy

I pull a blanket of darkness
to my chin and drift under the spell
of transformative dreams
while both sky and countryside
blink pinpoints of light

Flood

when I drowned
my lungs burned like fire.
dappled sunlight danced on the surface
I couldn't reach.
when I let go I was flooded with peace
and I thought of my mother.

several lifetimes later
someone saved my life.

Nocturne (Aura)

sometimes alone is empty
sometimes full.
I put on my robe and make tea,
moonlight floods the kitchen
and the snowy fields.
Night puts on her robe of stars,
down the road a yard light snaps on.
an aura of belonging,
a life happened here.

Nocturne (Starlings)

what shall become of me
heading through an unfamiliar door
to an unthinkable destination
yet something speaks to me
from a faraway place
something spinning at the edge
of my consciousness
an opening, a soft pull, a knowing
past regrets spin off and away
like a flock of starlings
who know where they're going

Moonlight

moonlight floods the kitchen
the refrigerator stands at attention
humming a tune
the furniture is alive at night
trancelike I wander the rooms
and enter a smoky mirror
full of ghosts
waiting for sleep, praying for sleep
last night I dreamed my hair was back
and I was happy and weightless

Nocturne (Compass)

when all is lost
what's left is the next step
images in the floating world
as I row toward an unfamiliar shore

I rise and rumble and roar
over edges, beginnings and endings
I pull a thread through my life
and everything vanishes behind it
This is the tipping point
my compass wobbles

II. Aubade

All Winter Long

all winter long
the geese flew overhead
in the high wild
would that I could call
into the wide open like them
my life is so large
miracles abound
as all morning I watch
a tiny spider spin its web
small patterns in a big world
cosmic design and the lightness
of being

Aubade (Bells)

my little life
no bigger than an ant's eye
yet more expansive and vast
than I know
memories ring round the edges
like distant bells

Lucky

it seems odd to feel lucky
about the cancer
the long wait for doctors
numerous tests and chemo
a shroud of uncertainty
and yet I feel fortunate
I get to stare death in the face
and stick my tongue out
I get to know deeply
how precious each day is
knowing nothing lasts

Aubade (Wheel)

everything is falling away,
falling away,
what I thought I knew,
what I thought I needed to know,
shadows and uncertainty,
things shift and fade and reappear—
friends, memories, health, dreams,
the great wheel of Samsara.

Childhood Scenes

stars, darkness, dreams, then oblivion
as I enter this world

a grandmother's comforting bosom
pajamas with feet
and a shadow wearing a stovepipe hat

at dawn the windows were on fire
it was only the sun
don't look in the closet

an old, abandoned chicken coop,
a small koi pond,
and an attic filled with old smells,
bats, and surprises

sheets flapping on a clothesline
like galleon sails
taking me far away

a vacant lot, a woodpile as a fort,
three huge willow trees
that grow with me

the great aunts in lawn chairs
in sour, flowered dresses,
they talk to me as if I'm real

Aubade (Quest)

In a parallel reality
I'm driving through Monument Valley
with the top down and
the wind in my hair.
I am full and unencumbered.
The Milky Way floats above
and around me.
I am on a quest
for my original self.

Spring

after the horse latitudes of winter
the long grey days,
spring roars in as a green engine
too early for others,
it's the tulips' domain,
grape hyacinth, daffodils, crocus,
their beauty and color a balm
to my soul,
later the allium and iris.
every spring I want to plant more.
I hardly ever do.
meanwhile, eternal return goes on.

Aubade (Stories)

what if I know who I am
  and why I'm here or not

what if I feel like an imposter and a sage
  at the same time

what if the trees know more than us
  and speak in their own language

what if everything we think we know is wrong
  and we don't know the half of it

what if the rocks tell stories that are
  millions of years old

what if God is exactly who we believe her to be
  and beliefs rule the way

what if God is beyond belief, opinion, dogma
  and rules, beyond certainty

what if eternity really exists and we're tumbled
  through lifetimes and dimensions

what if we're starlike beings
  shining backward and forward through
    all time

In a Dream

from the café window
I watch the world roll by
drinking in traffic as I sip chai tea

the day marches on
I wonder where people are going,
what they're thinking
how shall we fill this day, this life

the world floats by
in a dream

Aubade (Question)

sometimes the wind shifts to the north
and a strange crow pecks at my window

sometimes I orbit a darker star
sometimes medication helps

sometimes when the light pokes in
my shadow grows larger

sometimes earth forms quiet me
dragonflies, ferns, flowered fields

sometimes you can hear the trees moving
in a broad, soft sweeping whoosh

sometimes the geese fly so low
you can hear the air beneath their wings

sometimes petunias sing a petunia song
and petunia the air purple

sometimes the only question left
worth answering is
how may I serve?

Rainy Spring Day

a cold, rainy spring day
nevertheless the tree frogs
a woodpecker nearby
and the busy cardinals
calling back and forth
infinite forms of life pulsing
these sounds ring my day
with wonder, the world offers itself
Demeter returns from the underworld
and yes, life goes on
I notice this more and more
as I grow older
and closer to death
and dream of friends long departed

Aubade (Suitcase)

a cricket song this morning
as fog and mist from the long rain
shrouds the avenue.
today is as it is.

we go through our lives,
carrying a suitcase full of days,
dreams, joy and sorrow,
taking steps, moving forward,
standing still.
what is our purpose and destiny?
today is as it is.

Blackbirds

red-winged blackbird on a fencepost
in no particular hurry
as the world rushes by
all importance and urgency

I have nothing to say except
what the blackbird says
as I listen to the wind in the maples
and my own breathing

Aubade (Veil)

drinking in a drumming rain,
a soft lullaby made of water.
it softens me. I am fed,
and I drift between worlds,
weightless and unencumbered.
now is all there is.

Hafiz said there are plays
within plays that we cannot see.
other dimensions exist,
other connections invisible.
what does it matter to me
if a veil is lifted on the
timeless fabric of reality?

so much goes by unnoticed
in a day, in a life.
all we have is now.

Cloud Break

driving through town
when the clouds parted
and I felt whole and connected
to all that is,
grateful for compassionate friends
and all the world around me

this is how it is
in that sweet center spot
where it all comes together—
a responsibility to joy.
this is where we're meant to live.

Aubade (Song)

some day I will slip over
the edge of knowing
into other surprising realms

the cosmos sings us
in and out of being
our lives are the return song

I sing my body
  bone, blood, and breath
I sing the woodpecker in his red hat
I sing the rising moon
  ancient and radiant
I sing my friends beloved
  who have passed through my life
I sing the soil beneath the pavement
  longing for light
I sing the bear in her den dreaming
I sing the aurora borealis
  dazzling and hypnotic
I sing the many rooms of God's house

Above the Clouds

above the clouds and the rim
of the earth
stars arc in timeless distance

below the silent clouds
I will vanish one day
like a morning mist or dew

but in the world I will rise
we go on in some form
in the end, we are everywhere

in the chickadee's song
in a blue heron on an edge of pond
in the light on the leaf
and the worm in the bud
in the moon's bright passage
in the way your dog looks at you
in the pounding surf's roar and tug
in a trembling blade of grass
we are made to be part of everything

Aubade (Seedpod)

I collect seedpods, acorns, cones and such,
things opening and closing,
opening from a dark womb
to the startling light of belonging,
unfolding over and over.
This is how we save ourselves
and each other,
one pod at a time.

from Spin Infinity

Selected Poems

Reflection

the Universe has no center or edge.
it's the same with us,
rowing toward an illusion
of shore,
all the while knowing
we are both rower, and shore,
faint stars blinking
their million mile distance,
our reflection smiling
in a ring of water,
one circle among many.

Memo to Self

stop thinking so much.
you look for divinity everywhere
but inside yourself.

just to be is holy.
note the little breeze
and the wrens.

The Drifting

furiously the wind howls,
driving snow and debris before it.

gusts scream eerily through cracks.
pictures shudder on walls.

on nights like this I think
I have not loved enough,
I have not given as much as I could.

snow blows and drifts across fields.
that is what it does.

the wind roars and then is gone.
that is what it does.

they give themselves utterly, and move on.

[all the world's a driving wheel]

all the world's a driving wheel
across time and distance
there's no turning back
we shrink and expand
wander to come home

in another time I was that boy
hearing a locomotive whistle
its distance, getting closer and closer,
imagining faraway places, wild places,
places past the rim
of my understanding

what is the weight
of a nine-year-old's dreams
across time and space
there's no turning back

[depressed, crabby, moody]

depressed, crabby, moody,
chores piling up, worry wasting,
watching WW2 in color.
wind roars outside.
I want oblivion.
I want a deeper place to be,
I want to grow into the rest
of my life with abandon.
I want an opening to fly through.
This is why I listen to the birds.

[I am a black hole falling into myself]

I am a black hole falling into myself

I am a dream I had when I was 7

I am who I am and not
who I wanted to be

I am anti-depressants and feeling like
the color beige

I am what the trees said
when I wasn't listening

I am in the space between sentences
where God also resides

I am the field of sugar beets you're driving by
I am also what the bean field is not

I am disappearing down a road
rimmed with chicory and Queen Anne's lace

I am here and not here, everywhere
and nowhere at the same time

I am the dance of Shiva
and a flock of starlings lifting off

That humming sound
is just the world turning

[what does it mean to be here]

what does it mean to be here
  walking across the earth?
as my 64-year-old self drives north
  farms and furrowed fields float past.
I am alive in the world, alive in the world,
  breathing in, breathing out,
learning to let in and let go.

O God of All That Is
let judgment fall away,
  let my need for certainty fade.
I wonder at how the world
  keeps turning.
O for the Silent Center,
  let's just dance, let's just dance...

[it's an inch apart]

it's an inch apart,
the distance between
a wisp of spirit and weightlessness

between the beating heart
of a vole under snow
and a flutter of wings

between a mouthful of sand
and all the burning words
I never wrote or spoke

between the last breath
and the Light
that surpasses all

[act like you belong here]

act like you belong here.
act like you have a voice
and something to say
and the courage to say it!
your vision of how to be in this world
and what that means matters.

why are you so sad?
afraid to join the noisy world,
to participate.
it's all waiting for you
to open into it.
you're not separate.
rub up against the world,
step into it,
your destination is you.

[it was something I didn't know I knew]

it was something I didn't know I knew
everything was the same but different
and there was a sound that was
not a sound
more like a filling up
and everything hummed
and glowed from inside
I fell up into a kind of Grace
and all was Beloved
and all things became new
anything unresolved fell away
and all I felt was stars

[it was the music]

it was the music
that told the story

how a melody runs through everything
no louder than bees' wings

how the thread of things
runs through a lifetime

and you see how it all was and why
how the seasons fold into each other

meanwhile the asters
and rose of Sharon purple the air

as the music of spheres
sings my bones into words

[what if I told you]

what if I told you
it shines inside everything

there's no secret to living
every day is enough
ask the tree frogs, the foxglove
what they need to understand

across the world
bar-headed geese fly over
the Himalayas
a woman washes her clothes in a river
a pathway disappears

across the universe
of black holes and bumblebees
we spin in an infinity
disguised as daily life

ABOUT THE AUTHOR

LYNN RATHER lived in Michigan with her cats, rocks and fossils, perennial gardens, and a great love for poetry.

* 9 7 9 8 2 1 8 3 2 9 1 0 5 *